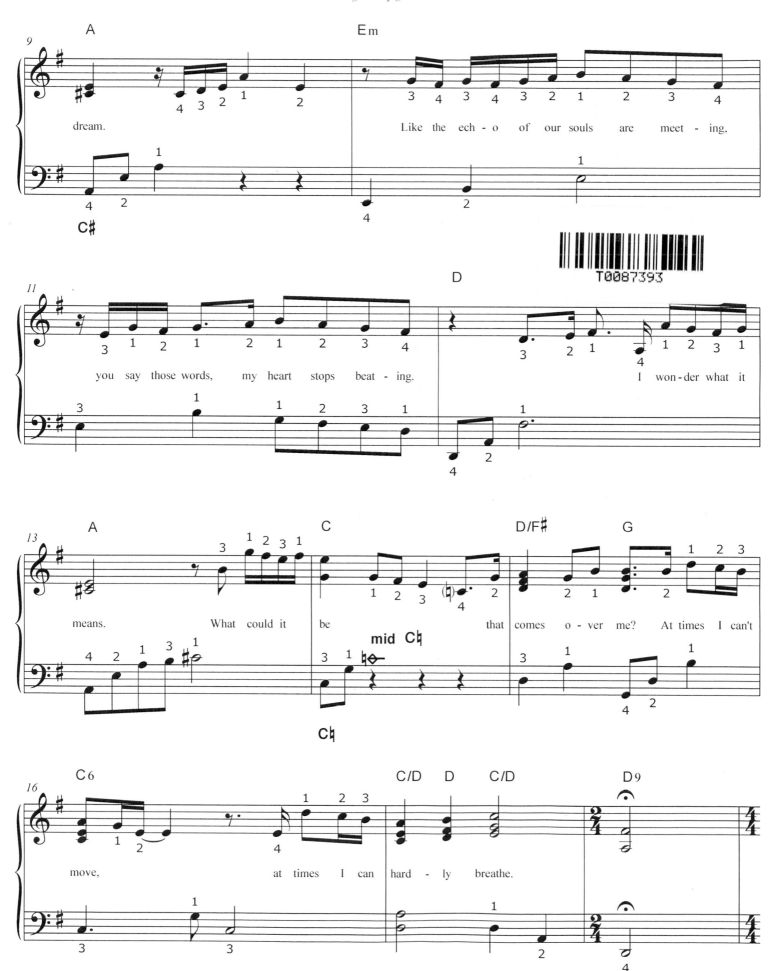

T0087393

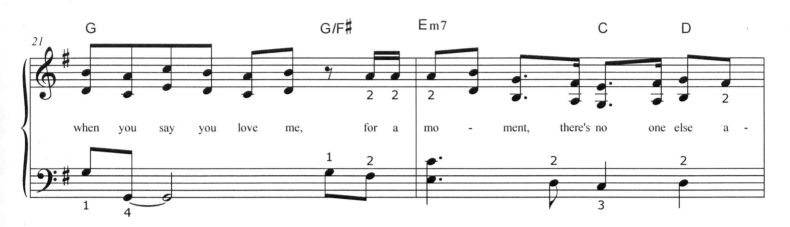

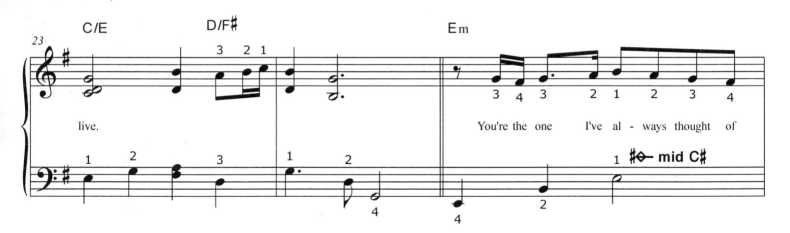

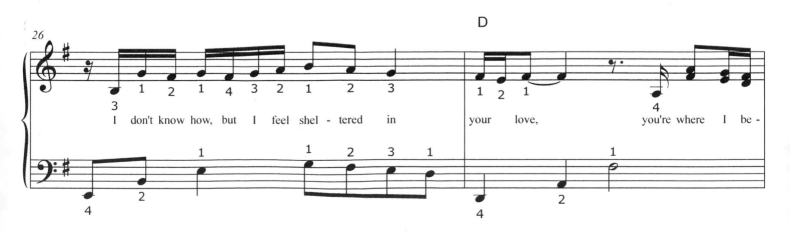

When You Say You Love Me

Words by Robin Scoffield
Music by Mark Hammond

Sharping lever changes are indicated with diamond notes and also with octave wording.
Pedal changes are written below the bass staff.

Be sure that the melody is always prominent. Accompaniment notes, particularly when in the right hand, should be lighter, and less important than the melody. You can use the lyrics to determine which notes are part of the melody.

When You Say You Love Me

Words by Robin Scoffield
Music by Mark Hammond

Harp arrangement by Sylvia Woods

You
Love
Me

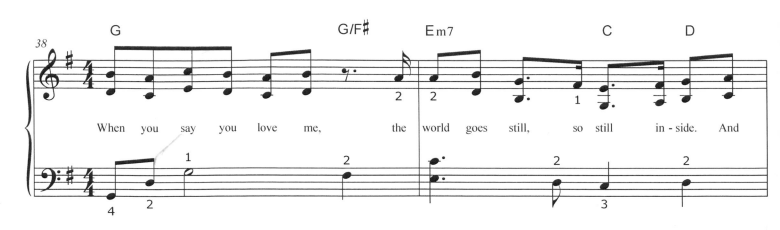

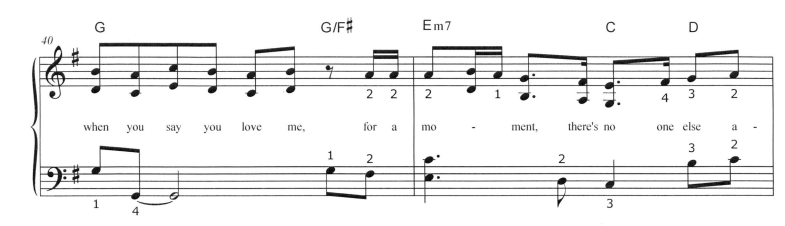

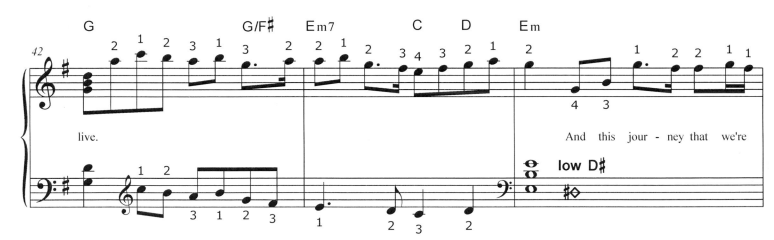

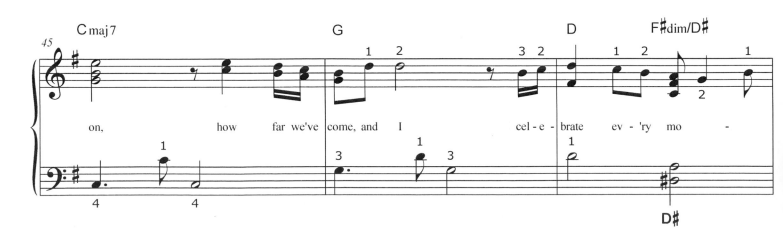

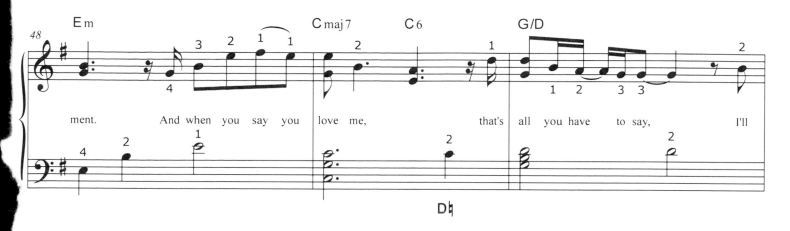

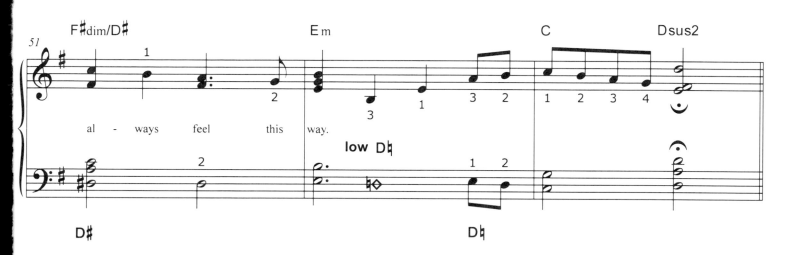

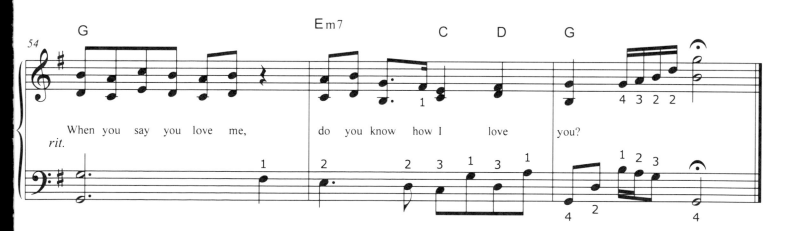

When You Say You Love Me

Josh Groban released his version of this song on his 2003 album "Closer."

More Harp Arrangements of Pop Music
by Sylvia Woods

Available from harp music retailers and www.harpcenter.com

Sylvia Woods Harp Center
P.O. Box 223434, Princeville, HI 96722 U.S.A.

ISBN-13: 978-0-936661-76-6

U.S. $7.95

HL00155943

EXCLUSIVELY DISTRIBUTED BY

HAL•LEONARD®
CORPORATION
7777 W. BLUEMOUND RD. P.O. BOX 13819
MILWAUKEE, WISCONSIN 53213

With many thanks to Paul Baker
and Denise Grupp-Verbon

© 2015 by Sylvia Woods
Woods Music & Books
P.O. Box 223434,
Princeville, HI 96722, U.S.A.

www.harpcenter.com